Signed, Sealed, Delivered

PURE LOVE SERIES

Denise Neal

AuthorHouse™
1663 Liberty Drive
Bloomington, IN 47403
www.authorhouse.com
Phone: 833-262-8899

This book is printed on acid-free paper.

ISBN: 978-1-6655-2463-6 (sc)
ISBN: 978-1-6655-2462-9 (e)

Library of Congress Control Number: 2021908856

Print information available on the last page.

Published by AuthorHouse 04/30/2021

Dedication

All glory and honor goes to my heavenly father. Thank you for giving me the words I need to express to others the love, you have shown and Given to me so freely and unconditionally.

Dove's Eyes

My eyes are as eyes of a dove, fixed firmly upon you.

You are the desire of my heart. My thoughts wrap around you like the warmth of a campfire, on a cold autumn night. My beloved, I take flight in your love; soaring high on the wings of an eagle! traveling roads that lead me straight back to you.

Song of Solomon 4:1

Warm Embrace

Oh! how I love you, let me count the ways. You wrapped me in your arms and brought me safely through the night.

I awoke in the warmth of your embrace, there is no one that could ever take your place. You bathe me in a love so sweet, the kind of love that won't melt in the heat; the kind of love that can't be beat.

Song of Solomon 2:14-17

The Presence Of Love

Rescuing me is something you do every day, it's the way you show me you're here to stay. When you enter the room, there's only you and I.

I get so high like a dove flying free in the wide open sky. In your presence, there's no greater blessing; than to be with you.

Song of Solomon 7:10-11

One Call Away

You're only one call away, you're always here to save my day. No one else compares to you, no one else can do the things you do. You show me you love me, even when I don'tdeserve it or when I feel I'm not worth it. You're never too far; always by my side. I don't need a phone, I just open my mouth and Say! thank you for being only one call away.

Jeremiah 23:23

Hearts Forever Intertwined

Even if I can't feel you and it feels as if you've forgotten about me, you reassure me that I'm always on your mind. All my fears melt away! because I know your love for me is here to stay. Like words engraved in a stone, it's forever! and I'm never alone.

Psalm 23:6

Yours Truly

You fight for me when the darkness causes me to lose sight of the love you have for me. You are my hero, my savior, you hold my hand as we walk in Victory.

Deuteronomy 20: 4

The Power Of Love

There are not enough words to describe your love for me. I can't even find the words to say; how you make my day in every way! tears of joy fill my heart like the sweet smell of fresh flowers every morning, like the taste of ripe juicy peaches; filling my taste buds with the sweet taste of goodness that never goes away. forever and always! is your love for me.

1 John 4:12

Unseen Beauty

My beloved,thank you for the smile you bring to my face; when I feel all hope is gone. You give me hope when everything feels hopeless, you fill my heart with joy when sadness tries to set in,you give me beauty for ashes. Your love is like no other to be compared to! the love you have for me is pure and true. I just want to say I love you.

Isaiah 61:1-3

My Beloved

I am my beloved's and beloved is mine. Oh how wonderful are you to me. Your love is as leaves, when it changes into the beautiful bold and bright colors of the Autumn season. How Wondrous to behold, so warm and inviting! I forget about the cold. Old things passed away but your love remains the same. Things I thought were dead, are breathing new like again! you cause your love to shine on the darkest places, you are the one my heart adores. I am my beloved's and his desire is towards me.

Song of Solomon 6:3,6,10

Flowers

Thank you my love, for the flowers. In an hour when it was much needed, when I was down; you brightened my day and lifted my spirit. Thank you my love for the flowers. Your love for me goes beyond the highest tower, deeper than the ocean, wider than the sky.

I let out a sigh in awe of you because your love for me is un-describable.

Song of Solomon 6:2

Hand Of Love

I am bathed in the warmth of your love as I feel the sweet caress of your patient hands.

I can feel it's embrace, from the Top of my head to the tips of my toes; always here beside me! ever so close. Holding me tightly, never letting go. Always and forever is the promise you made, even when I'm not deserving! you never throw shade.

Joshua 1:9

Eternal Flame

Your love for me is as a burning flame, that many waters can not quench; neither can the flood drown it. Burning brightly and strong! searing my heart, making me forever yours.

Song of Solomon chapter 8:6-7

Pursuit of Love

I see your passion for me, in everything you do for me. I clearly see your love for me, it settles all my curiosities. No longer have to wonder; things that plunder my heart, is no longer so. The love you show me, raises me up from the low places.

Psalm 4:7

You Love Me

Because you love me, I always win. In spite of what I've done or where I've been, your arms are always open for me to walk right in; because you love me. So at the end of the day, and everything is said and done; I long to feel your warm embrace. A love like no other, a love pure and true, a love that's always there, to bring me through.

Jeremiah 31:3

Perfect Love

Your love is like unto a fountain, that flows free and never ending. A perfect love, that found me! setting my spirit free. Your love is as deep as the rolling sea; it runs to the most forgotten, it runs for eternity. A love that says I'm free, a love that belongs to me.

Romans 8:38-39

Forever Abiding

You're always here with me. I never have to wonder where you are or search very far. My beloved knows what I need, he knows how I feel inside. With him I don't have to pretend and never need to hide. My beloved always keeps his word and Promises to always abide with me.

1John 4:15-17

Sweet Aroma Of Love

You carry my heart in your tender loving hands and care for it, as if it's Your own! with a loving kindness I've never known.Your love is as the sweet aroma of the finest perfume, the only one who's noticed as you enter the room. Ever so quiet yet so strong. When things are out of place in my world you carefully put them back where they belong; always reminding me oh! how you love me.

2 Corinthians 2:15

Two Hearts Beating As One

Joy fills my heart when I'm with you! all I can do is run into your arms. Your love draws me closer to you, like a moth to a flame! my heart you claimed from the start. We will always be a part of each other. There is no me without you.

1 Corinthians 6:17

Endless Love

You took my heart and caused everything in me to change, that's why I spend every day in love with you.You took my life and made it beautiful, Your love holds me close and never lets me go. It's your love that gives me strength every morning. It's your love that makes me free. All this Joy, there's no way I can hide it! It's your love and I must talk about it.

1 Peter 4:8

Overcomer

you made me lighter, all my worries are gone.Your love keeps taking me higher. It's given me the strength I need to believe, I can do all things; because You love me. Every time I hear your voice, every time you speak the words it reminds me again! that life is worth living, because You love me and that's enough! you love me.

Psalm 28:7

Love's Delight

How beautiful is your love. Oh! like the work of fine jewels that no one will ever comprehend. How fair and pleasant you are, loves' delight! as all manner of pleasant fruit; your love is glorious to behold.Your Banner over me is love.

Song Of Solomon 2:1-5

In Love's Embrace

Your love raises me up and takes me away to places I've never been before, where flowers appear and the time of singing birds is come. A love that speaks to me and says; arise my love, my fair one and come away with me.

Song Of Solomon 2:10-13

One Word

My prince, my love, my everything! one word will never be enough to describe who you are to me. One word will never be enough to express how you make me feel; it's like a new experience each and every day, more than words could say. It's incredible how you make my day.

Song of Solomon 1:14

Isaiah 5:1

Love Uncontained

My mind keeps trying to understand; what only my spirit can. A love so great, A love so deep! I can feel it all around me. never selfish, always kind; the kind of love that continues to blow my mind.

Jeremiah 31:3

Love's Light

You are the breath I take, the air I breathe; you are my everything.
You're like my first cup of tea in the morning, you give me the strength
I need to get through.Your love keeps me going when there's no reason
to. Your love heals my broken heart; delivers me from the sadness I
hold so deep inside. You wrap me in your love so tight; the darkness
can no longer hide. I am free in your light.

John 1:5

Isaiah 60:1

Smile

You make me happy, you take the pain away and put a smile on my face. Because you live! I live! you make me whole; I'm so in love with you. Just the thought of you puts a smile on my face, a smile that won't go away, a smile that can't be erased; always have to stay.

Nehemiah 8:10

Never Alone

My beloved is always with me, I'm never alone. You call me all your own. With you, I never have to wonder where I belong. In a world filled with hate there's no debate about your love for me. I feel

It when I rise in the morning, I feel it when I'm resting in your inviting arms.

Psalm91

Love chose me

You make living in this world easier, I don't need to jump through hoops or compete In any way for you. Your love for me is like the taste of the sweetest cherries bursting in my mouth, making me want to savor every moment. Like the supple feel of the morning dew, resting upon a velvet red rose.

I am the one you chose.

John15:16

You Touched my Heart

My beloved, you touched my heart. You touched my heart as only you can, my knees buckled to the floor; your love trickled down to the very core of my being. You're always sure to blow my mind each and every time.

Proverbs 23:26

Psalm 37:4

Treasured Love

You're on my mind from the time I wake up in the morning, until the going down of the sun.

My day isn't done until I spend time with you. You make my day complete only then can I finally sleep. You are apart of me, the love we share goes deeper than anyone will see; or even comprehend. You and me together is the way it's always been. My eyes are now opened.

2 Corinthians 4:6-7

Walking in destiny

Love is our destiny, there's no other way it could ever be! pure as a dove swooping down to rest upon me like the morning dew resting upon a pink silky rose penetrating deep giving much needed nourishment. Your love causes me to bloom.

1thessalonians 3:12

Ephesians 4:15

Special

You make me feel like I'm the only one for you. You focus in on me when I need you to. Like the eyes of a dove and strength of an eagle, you watch for me and only me.

You watch for me, to keep me safe from all who seek to harm me. Special I am to you.

You will always pursue me, because you love me.

Zechariah 2:8

Love Beyond Borders

In times of unrest and times of being uncomfortable, I find comfort in you. You know just what to do to calm my spirit and take away the fear. You cause me to understand things I never did before. With much patience and kindness, you cause me to soar; to places I never been before. Your love for me causes me to pay attention to things I use to Ignore, putting a desire in me to explore further and deeper! beyond Borders.

Psalm 32:7-8

Exodus 33:14

Love To The Rescue

There's never been a moment, where I'm not thinking of you. My hopelessness is gone because you love me. Where I have been broken; my innocence stolen!

you came and rescued me. When I can't speak a word, I let out a deep breath; you hear my SOS. You find me in the middle of my darkest night, it's true! you rescue me. There is no distance where you can not find me; you cover me over and over again. Because you Love me, I'm not defenseless.You are my hiding place, you keep me safe from all hurt,harm and danger.

2 Samuel 22:17-20

Psalm 18:16-19

Still Here

You've seen me at my best, you've seen me at my worst! and you're still here. In times when I didn't care, in times when I've walked in fear;

You loved me! in spite of and you're still here. Still here; guiding and protecting me. Still here! hovering over me like a dove with your love. I hear the sweet whisper of your words, assuring me that everything will be okay; like a baby cub cuddled up in Mama bears arms, you wrapped me in your love and I'm safe from all harm.You're still here because you promise that you will never leave me nor forsake me. I belong to you, no one is able to take me away from you.

John 10:28-29

Hebrews 13:5

My Heart Beats For Only You

My heart beats for you and only you. I never met anyone like you. So kind, so true! my heart beats for only you. This world is empty, pale and void compared to knowing you my love. Sometimes I say no and try to let go of you but you hold on to me, no matter what I do.

My heart beats for you and only you.Through all my doubt and fear you continue to assure me that your love is true.

Jeremiah 31: 3-4

1Samuel 16:7

The focus Of Love

The apple of your eye, is what I am to you. I am the center of your focus, every little thing I do you take notice. My purpose is to love you; nothing else matters. My heart is no longer shattered, because of you. You caused my heart to beat again.

Psalm 17:18

I give you my heart

My heart is wide open for you. Your arms are stretched always to receive me. You won't let me down, you won't break my heart, you won't let me fall; so I give you my heart. I present my life to you, you always take the time to make me smile.

Jeremiah 31:3

Love Shining Through
The Window

You freely give your love to me, all of your love. Your love is like the dance of a graceful swan gliding across a pond perfect, flawless, one of a kind. Your love shines upon me, like the sun shining through a window pane; wide open for the world to see! with no guilt or shame.

2 Corinthians 4:6

Strength In Love

Your love is strength to my spirit. Your love has made me strong.

Now I can do anything!

because of your love, I am unstoppable. There's no way I can lose; I can do anything

beyond what I can see.

You make me want to be all that I can be.

Psalm 46:1-2

Real Love

You are like no other I've known before. It amazes me, how you love me; the way you do. Everyday with you is like a brand new song, like the morning dew; so refreshing and new. It never gets old, it never gets boring. I'm your princess, you are such a prince but this is not a fairytale; this is real! and it will last until the end of time.

1 Corinthians 14: 4-8

1 John 4:16

You

My one true and only beloved.

I turn to you because you are my shelter, in the storm. In you! I do live, move and have my being. I'm nothing without you. You are a part of every moment of my life. You calm my raging sea, you walk with me through the fire and mend my broken Heart. You are all I need.

Psalm 46:1-2

The Great Beyond

Now! nothing is impossible.

You hold my world in Your hands; your love for me expands Beyond borders, beyond what the eye could see. my mind can't comprehend; it's beyond belief! how much you love me.

Ephesians 3:19

Love Worth Dying For

Your love pierce my heart like a sharpened knife cutting through a sweet delicate piece of fruit. Feeling unworthy of it, but everyday you show me I'm worth it. You said I was to die for, you made my heart soar. You pour your love into me, never want to be without you.

Isaiah 53:3-5

1 Peter 3:18

Thoughts Of Love

Your love causes me to do things that seem impossible with your love, I'm unstoppable.

Your love is remarkable. I could climb the highest mountain, swim the deepest sea; your love is keeping me above all the darkness so I can clearly see

Psalm 119:105

John 8:32

The Power Of Love

Always watching over me, making sure I'm always free; leaving no space for the enemy. Unseen danger in this place but I have no need to worry in any case. Your love covers me and danger is afraid and only wishes to hide its face.

Psalm 91

Love Me Like You Do

Always loved! never forgotten, never discarded; like a rotten piece of fruit that has lost its flavor and no longer any use. I'm always wanted, forever needed. I don't need a reason for you to love me like you do.

Romans 5:8

Zephaniah 3:17

Strength

You are my strength, strength like no other. Your love reaches for me; like the warmth of a fireplace filling the room on a cold winter's night, like a hand extending its help to pull me up when I'm stuck and feeling all alone. Safe in your love is where I belong.

Exodus 15:2

Not Without Me

You love me! past what the eye can see. I'm where you want to be; I belong to you and you belong to me. Fear has no dominion over destiny. Our love is destined; from the beginning, now and forever. There's no greater love than this, heavenly bliss.

Matthew 28:20

Untouched Love

Although we can not touch physically! you touch my heart with the things you do for me.

You listen when I speak, go to war for me; spiritually. This love you have for me just can't be beat. When I have no words; you speak for me. I am a princess who has found her prince. A story that doesn't seem to make any sense; a story that can't be comprehended in the natural Sense.

1 Peter 1:8

Defining Love

I'm nothing without you,

You define my identity. I now have the strength to believe life is worth living; because you love me! because you love me, I can go anywhere; do anything! whatever my mind can obtain.

No limits, no boundaries. Your love gives me what I need to believe.

Jeremiah 31:3

Treasures

I'm shining like a diamond because you took the time to find me, in a darkness that tried so hard to confine me. I'm a precious stone that can't be owned by anyone but you.

1 Peter 2:9-10

Greater In Me

There's greater in me, something only you can see.

Something powerful, something that could change the world;

Emerging from the deepest depths, things that were kept

and unrealized. You said the time is now! Bringing forth what was bound, chains hitting the ground. Now free to be what my beloved expects of me.

1 John 4:4

Sight Unseen

Hands up, heart open wide;

I surrender all! to you, my beloved. Let everything else fade away. Something has to break, I need to see your face.

Darkness tries to erase every trace of you; so that I won't have anything to hold on to.

My beloved resumes me and set me free, if only they could see; how things really are! and not what seems to be; allow themselves to be captured in a love unconditionally.

2 Corinthians 5:7

Love Conquers All

You love me unconditionally, you don't stop talking to me inconveniently. I don't have to wonder how to be!

around you; it just comes naturally. You are my comforter, I am an overcomer because of you. I spend my days unsure about everything but you remind me that I am a conqueror. You love me, and that helps me to understand! your plan for me; is what's best for me.

Romans 8:37

Hero

In the midst of the storm, your love is still strong. Pushing me on; beyond limits and borders, beyond what my mind can see. You make me believe I can do anything. You hear my call; when situations get too tall for me to handle, like a mountain I cannot climb. You're the hero that never leaves my side.

Matthew 19:26

Deuteronomy 31:6

Philippians 4:13

Picture Perfect Love

It's so pure; untainted. Like a picture perfect painting, unflawed. Your love for me; is what I'm speaking of. You love me without conditions. so many things I don't understand, but knowing you love me and protect me; fear doesn't stand a chance.

1 John 4:16

Colossians 3:14

Wonderful Love

Something wonderful happened deep on the inside of me; that can now be seen on the outside. Your Love causes me to shine bright; it brings light to the dark places, I didn't even know were there. It tears through the deepest wounds, penetrates my heart until there's no room for everything else but more of you.

Proverbs 4:18

Abiding, Uncontained Love

Your love takes a hold of me!

like a fire, like a flood it can't

be contained. Bursting from the seams; beams of light shining through. A love so pure, a love so true; it makes everything brand new. It can't be bought or exchanged for anything! It claimed me for its own. A love I never knew I needed, a love I never thought existed.

Isaiah 41:13

Psalm 23

Timeless

Glowing on the inside and it's showing on the outside; so bright! it can not hide. Love illuminating, love penetrating deep like space between the earth and the sky; I see no end in sight. like fresh flowers that bloom year after year; your love continues to sear my soul. Oh! how you love me and care for me, a love that never gets old.

Psalm 136

Better

You and I have history; we go way back. From the beginning of time, I was yours and you were mine. It doesn't matter what people say, it doesn't matter what they think! I love you anyway. You are good, you are good to me; you have always been faithful to remind me of your love. Consistent Through the ages! you keep on getting better.

Daniel 7:9-10,13-14

True Story

You'll never leave me; because you love me. From the rising of the sun, until the going down of the same; we will forever remain one, even after this life is done. Our paths were never our own, my heart is yours and your heart is mine. We'll tell our own story! hand in hand one step at a time.

Isaiah 41:13

Joshua 1:9

Blooming Love

I flourish! like bright flowers blooming in spring. Like birds singing sweet songs in a garden; Joy springing up in the morning. The beauty of your love surrounding me; like rivers flowing with no end. Your love inviting me to come on in; like the warmth of home, like the sweet taste of savory apple pie; your love abides with me forever.

Psalm 136:1-3

Love Carries Me Through

My soul can't live without you. It's like a heart without a beat, like a ship without a sail. Everything I do without you I fail. Your love keeps me strong and steady; ready to explore uncharted territory. Places I've never thought possible, places I never thought I'd go. Your love is taking me there. My heart fills with joy to know you're always there and I can share every moment with you.

Romans 10:17-18

Ephesians 2:10

Love's Search

I've been searching for someone who will fight for me, someone who will see me through. My knight in shining armor; that's you. I don't have to search no further because you're the one yes! you're the One. You're all I've been searching for, it's you I adore. Your love pours into me like a steady stream, a never ending road that goes way Beyond what the eye can see. Your love makes the possibilities unless. I am in this with you forever.

Luke 15:10

Flow

Your love flows through my soul; like blood flows through my veins a necessity! must have, like a light illuminating and guiding me down a dark path. Without your love I will lose my way, like an out-of-control car falling into the bay; Holding on to you for dear life. Your Love flows through my soul keeping me close and holds me tight.

John 17:16

Beyond Dreams

Your love for me is so strong! so deep, You show yourself to me as I sleep. Visions so lovely and sweet, so real so complete. My dreams can't compete with your love; it goes beyond the things I dream of. Though we're far apart! we are one; one soul, one spirit nothing is able to penetrate it.

John 4:7-8

Genesis 2:19

Protection

You protect me beyond what I can see, it's beyond belief how much you love me. You protect me with your warmth and tenderness. Your love takes away all the bitterness I felt inside. Now! all that remains; all that abides is you. You're inside me keeping me alive, like a heart that beats steady; your love doesn't skip a beat. It causes me to rest easy.

2 Thessalonians

Proverbs 18:10

Psalm 5:11

Just The Way I Am

You love me just the way I am. I don't need to fake, floss or pretend. I don't need to change anything! because you love me just the way I am. You love the way my eyes sparkle as the rays of the sunlight bounces off of them, you love the way my eyebrows are shaped even though they're barely there. You love me inside and out; you understand what I'm all about. I have no doubt about your love for me.

Philippians 3:7-21

2 Peter 1: 10-11

Forever Yours

No worries to speak of, all I have to do is look above. Your love shines upon me like the sun shines upon the earth; covering me with warmth, kissing me with kindness; always there! even when I can't see it. My gray skies are now blue. You are true to me and only me, where I am is where you want to be; forever and always.

Romans 14:18

1 Timothy 1:17

John 3:1-24

No Words

You're always watching over me, because I don't see everything. When I'm feeling all alone you make it a point to show me that you're right by my side, in you! I can always confide. Never alone; don't have to hide inside myself. I don't need no one else because I have you. When I don't know how to communicate or have the words to say, one word from you makes it all okay.

Isaiah 43

You Never Lie

You never lie to me. You are as true as true can be. You satisfy me when there seems to be no relief. Weeping in my soul, everything around me feels cold; feels like I'm frozen, can't feel the love inside; told by those close to me. Is this a dream or is this reality? because sometimes the way I feel! confuses me. You never lie to me; confidence and security is what you give to me.

Titus 1:2

Hebrews 6:18

Numbers 23:19

That's Love

Your loving kindness every morning! that's love. The flowers you give me to lift my spirit, that's love. The word you whisper in my ear; telling me I can do anything, go anywhere! that's love. I'm your one and only; the only one you're thinking of, that's love. You correct me when I'm wrong and still make me feel like I belong, that's love. The actions you take; not only the words you say! keeps me safe and secure, that's love.

1 Corinthians 13:4-8

Printed in the United States
by Baker & Taylor Publisher Services